G000255274

A Landscape of GRIEF

Forty Reflections for the Journey

JENNY HAWKE

DARTON · LONGMAN + TODD

First published in 2023 by
Darton, Longman and Todd Ltd
1 Spencer Court
140 – 142 Wandsworth High Street
London SW18 4JJ

ISBN: 978-1-915412-23-2

A catalogue record for this book is available from the British Library.

Designed and produced by Judy Linard

Printed and bound by Replika Press Pvt Ltd, India

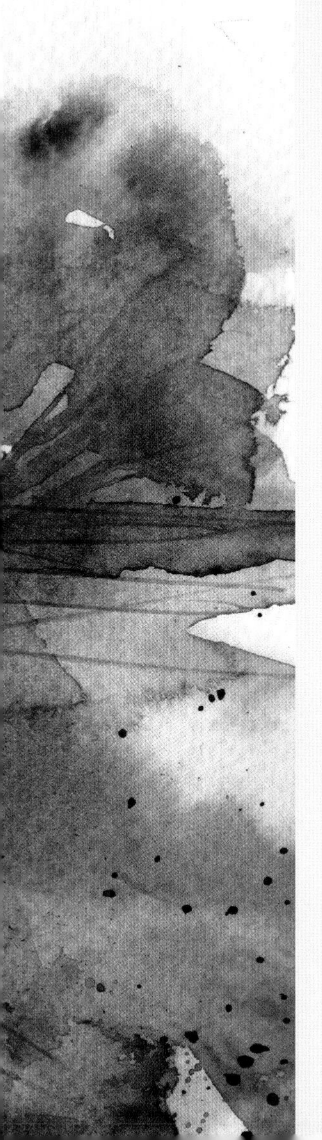

Contents

For Peter,
the love of my life

Introduction

Why I wrote this book

In many ways this book is a tribute to my husband. Peter was a kind and loving man, generous with all he had; thinking of others so often before himself, he was endlessly curious about life and about the people he met. He loved his family and only wanted us to be happy. He made endless puns which wore me out but the rest of the family loved him for it. He was a teacher, mentor, and writer. He loved learning and so lived a full and busy life. We all believed we would have him for so much longer. When he became ill our lives changed radically, so this book is my story, our story, of a marriage interrupted by a disease. A story of how day followed day through three years of not knowing if we could survive it. A story of losing the love of my life, of grieving the loss of him and the loss of my faith, and of faith rediscovered, and of how life carries on even when I didn't wish it to.

But above all this is a story of honest and raw emotion, honest experience of the darkest of times, and honest comment on how we can help each other as we grieve. There is darkness and there is light, and whilst we grieve we walk between the two. This is, as you may have discovered for yourself, a new landscape in which you find yourself. The roads ahead are unfamiliar. There are no signs to point the way, unless someone else has been there before you. And those of us who have cannot tell you the right way, the best way to grieve, but we can talk of how we found our own way, and how we kept breathing and moving in spite of ourselves in the hope it might bring you some peace. Step by step. Day by day.

How to use this book

This is a book to be journeyed through slowly. Perhaps because you are grieving. Perhaps because you want to connect with faith again through your pain. And perhaps because there is much food for thought, and ways in which this book can be a kindness for your soul. If you are grieving, you do not need fixing. You do not need to 'get through this' or 'to let go'. Your grief is yours, and there are no road maps for how you adjust to this new landscape – so please, take your time. Sit with the words, absorb the colours and know there is no rush for this.

And if you know someone who is walking this landscape, you may find new ways to help and care for them, as you walk with them.

PART ONE

This, our story

1. It began with a smile

How strange. Looking back, it all began with a smile. The first sign. The left side of his face was drooping. Only very slightly but it was there. I watched him on and off over the next few weeks, not wanting to admit there was anything wrong. Denial is a powerful thing. And, as we found out later, a useful tool. In the end I asked him. 'Does your face feel ok?' He said it was fine but asked why. I minimised the symptoms and suggested it might be a Bell's Palsy. We would watch for a while. But then he noticed certain letters were difficult to pronounce. As if his mouth was on a different time clock to his brain. I began to feel worried. My physio brain kicked in. A mini stroke. Or something worse.

We ignored it and watched it in uneasy turns, neither of us wanting to admit there might be anything seriously wrong. But in the end, reality pushed denial to the edges of our fragile cocoon and we had to take action. The GP looked kind but serious. No, it wasn't a Bell's Palsy. No, it couldn't be his damaged neck, or a mini stroke. We needed to be referred, and with that our hearts sank, as if weighted by a rock and thrown against our will into the deepest pond of dread.

I knew. I knew. As a physio, I knew. And I carried it for months. I researched. There was nothing else it could be. No point speaking my fears to Peter or the children, so I became an expert liar. I held it to myself until there was no hiding anymore. The consultant was kind.

And so gentle, as the diagnosis was spoken. 'I think you have Motor Neurone Disease. The bulbar type which affects speech, swallowing, and breathing.'

Neither of us moved. Expectation is a strange bedfellow. I had imagined I would cry, even lose control. I thought Peter would weep. But no. We sat numb to the core. A slow realisation that there was little else to say.

'Do you have any questions?'

Yes. We needed space, desperate to replay those few seconds and not have those words spoken over us again. We wanted to be told all would be well. For him to say to us there was a cure. But there wasn't. The meeting over, we were shown into the waiting room, already full of very sick people. People like us. I begged a passing nurse through the tears, which now came in full flood, for a room where we could sit quietly. Just to be apart from other people's reality. She found a small white room, more like a cupboard, and there we held each other. Peter wept. I tried to calm my heart, fluttering wildly inside me as if trying to find a desperate escape for us both, but there was none. Then cold calm came over me. We walked out. A tenuous suggestion of three years, maybe more, had been delivered by the consultant, reluctant to compound our mounting pain.

'Go live your life,' he said.

On the way home we discussed telling our son and daughter. Should we wait until our son's engagement meal in two days' time was over?

Could we pretend all was well? In the end we knew we were not that strong. That evening was the hardest thing we'd ever had to face. To tell your son and daughter their father has a terminal disease, there are few words to describe how we felt as their worlds broke apart that day.

'I'm so sorry. Dad is really sick.'

The three of them huddled on the sofa in a tangle of arms and tears, faces buried into each other whilst I wept again, standing near, on guard, as if it might make a difference.

The next days blurred into an unreality we were desperate to escape. Family and friends voiced their shock, but we were in a distant bubble, careering into an orbit which was out of control. No one could reach us.

And so it began.

Some time later, having been approached by a seemingly heartless medical student who wondered if I might like to write a journal on 'the carer's journey' (I did not respond well to this careless and brutal request), I decided that I would never ever document the progress of this disgusting and destructive disease. I would not give it airtime. I could hardly bear to write its name. Rather, we would navigate this sea together, deciding to deny its inevitability, and live to the full, until forced unkindly otherwise. I would write when it was over. Enough now just caring for him.

2. Before time runs out

You do what you've always wanted to do. You look at your bucket list. You stop dreaming and start doing. We'd always loved Swanage, holiday home for years to our children, who slotted in to the world of beaches, sandcastles and Grandma's cooking, as only happy kids can do. We followed suit for so many countless and joy-filled years. We dreamt of owning a property there but never found the courage or the time. Yet, that same devastating week, my daughter started looking. She found a small cottage which looked like a home from home. Two days later, Peter, Jessamy, and I, stood outside this stone terraced house, wedged in between even older properties, any doubts as to what the future held firmly ignored. The door opened and I knew we were home. This was the gift. Unwarranted, undeserved. I felt like God had poured out this bucketful of blessing onto our heads simply because we so desperately needed it. It made none of our current truth any easier but it was a magical gift. I rang my son, who was both incredulous and bemused at the news but joyful too. Our offer was accepted within two hours and we moved in within three weeks due to the estate agent's kindness. 'Oh, and there's an artist's studio at the top of the garden too,' he said. Almost too much to bear. Happiness mixed like oil and water with the painful truth that this was to be enjoyed now. This was our present in both senses of the word. The only one we had. We shut the world out and looked to the coming summer.

A Landscape of Grief

3. The bad news, always the bad news

It seems that me that the medical profession is trained to always point out the worst. The bad news. To tell you before you've even asked what is coming next. Every three months we would go back to the same consultant who would begin to tell us what Peter was going to lose next, the assumption being that you hadn't done any research yourself, or that you really wanted to know every grim detail of how this was going to get even worse. I guess I understand that in some situations this might be necessary, but I realised early on that it was robbing us of any hope of slowing this down. We knew there was little hope but we wished to stay in the present for as long as we could, so we politely said no, we haven't watched the video. No, we don't want to watch the insertion of a feeding-tube. No, please, just let us be for today. We know what's coming.

4. Peter's choice

It was the way he always lived. His principles, his strongest values, these were what drove him. Justice, compassion, honesty, kindness, fun, and, above all, service to others. He chose to simply carry on as he had done before, looking for ways he could support us, and helping others find their perfect job, writing programmes for people who felt stuck in their own lives.

And so the days began to pass, an uncertain reality always the backdrop to whatever we did or said. There was little of note to see at first. He made up his mind to ignore the progress of the disease as much as he could. Hope came in sunburst flashes. New research from other countries, new ways to approach the future. Prayers were said, both boldly and with quiet desperation in turns, until the power of words left the house and left my heart. We felt abandoned in small and large ways as we watched each other bearing this new burden. Trying to protect each other, a quiet tension entered our lives. Anger and hope played hide and seek like fast companions whilst we waltzed around each other. Sometimes his anger spilled over, affecting us all with the depth of his frustration at losing his speech and so much more. People treated him differently. On a train, we were stared at. In a café, we were always watched. Questions were put to me rather than to him, the assumption being that because he looked increasingly different, he therefore couldn't understand. I did not react well to this. He simply shrugged his shoulders.

But, and this is an enormous but, he simply carried on. He wrote. He kept running the job club until it was no longer tenable. He walked, he exercised, he cycled, he ate well, and somehow, somehow, he still showed his love for us. In short, he took control, challenging this disease to run on in the face of his enormous strength. And most of all, he refused to get depressed. He talked in the early days of a conversation he had with his mother. She had been losing her sight over several years but had refused to accept she was going blind, always losing her glasses though she had many pairs. One day, Peter asked her how it was that she wasn't depressed. She replied, in that very matter-of-fact way, 'What on earth good would it do to get depressed?'

The conversation ended there, but she remained his quiet and extremely dogged inspiration. Life went on, we did our best, and he lost what little control he had over his body. Inch by painful inch.

5. The hospice, a place of peace

The day came, as I knew it would, when Peter could no longer eat or drink. The hospice welcomed us to the strangeness of this chapter of our lives. We were shown into the room that was to be our home for whatever future we had. A bed, chairs, cupboard, bathroom, and French doors opening out on a view of a sweet garden. And there was a large whiteboard on the wall for us to write our names on, and Peter's likes and dislikes, and the names of friends who were coming to visit. After a while the nurse returned to see if we were ok. I said that in a strange way it felt like we were in a four-star hotel. Quick as a flash Peter typed out on his keyboard a potential Trip Advisor review: 'A hotel to die for!'

He would have smiled if he could!

And that was the man I loved and lived with for forty-two years. An acid sense of humour such that, even when confronted with the end of his life, he could make a joke of it all. We wrote his comment on the white board where it remained for the rest of our stay.

A Landscape of Grief

Peter could no longer swallow but one of the nurses quickly told him he could have a sponge dipped into water or alcohol to keep his mouth from getting dry. He had always loved whisky so he sent out text messages and copious emails to the friends who wanted to join us, saying that they could only gain entry to our room if they came bearing a bottle of whisky. And he meant it. After a few days had passed the room smelt like a brewery, and every surface and shelf was covered by a laughable number of bottles. I think we counted thirty in all. So the days passed by in a murky haze of whisky-flavoured air, laughing and crying with friends who drank on his behalf, while the nurses simply smiled and carried on with their sacred work.

He even woke me up at 5.30 one morning to pour him his first glass of the day, and I didn't blame him for that. Small things. We need to celebrate them all, even in the face of death.

What follow now are excerpts of my diary which I posted each day on my social media. It was a therapy for me, both in acknowledging what was happening and in staying in touch with the wider world as much as I felt able. It chronicles the waves of emotion, the craziness of beloved friends, the memories we made, and the quiet acceptance that this was it. We were losing him.

A Landscape of Grief

PART TWO

The diary begins

I have written every day for the last seven years. It started as a challenge to myself and then it became a happy necessity for me. I have slowly begun to realise the importance of telling your story in whatever way you choose, and even if you're not sure anyone will read it. It's your story and it matters. And this book is mine. As you read this first entry here, you need to imagine you are welcomed with us in our hospice room. Peter is centre stage, and the room is full of friends and beloved family. Even our scruffy dog Mortimer is with us. Whisky bottles, mostly half drunk, line every available surface. The gentle company of nurses is with us too, anticipating our needs and rejoicing in this, our final party. And an undercurrent, as always, of a holy presence, reminding us that this is indeed palpable and holy ground. We stand on the border, a thin line between earth and sky. A thin place.

And now, as I read through these diary entries, I am aware of so many other things I want to say. My hope for you is that somehow these thoughts might make your journey a little smoother. I can do nothing to lighten your load but I can show you a few fresh footsteps ahead which may be an easier reach for you right now. We who are a little way ahead of you call out to you quietly. You are not alone. Read on.

1. Yesterday we partied

So yesterday we partied. In the Hospice. We saw old friends, reminisced, and fell about laughing at the old and not-so-old stories of youth and middle age. We drank whisky and gin, and ate gingerbread and chocolate. We blew bubbles at each other, we sang loudly, and we broke bread together. We cried and hugged, and some of us said our farewells. What a day. And in hindsight an incredible privilege.

It strikes me that each day we live should hold a moment of intensity, however small and fleeting it may be. A space where we see and recognise our significance through the eyes of others, where we feel so intensely that we know again we are alive, and so we celebrate our living.

Sometimes we don't appreciate that significance until the day is done, but no matter. We learn to treasure each memory of those times, like gifts from another existence. Gifts to be held when times are dark and the shadows intense. Our hands may be empty but they hold so much love. That is a fragment of comfort for us today.

2. His final day

And so we sit. Activity finally slowing. Ice-cold drink. Mouthwash on a sponge. Bed up. Bed down. Covers on. Covers off. Cooling flannel on the forehead. Friends to visit and say their goodbyes. Tears mixed with bittersweet laughter, the oddest of companions. Prayers, anger, confusion, and icy calm. This has been so strange a journey. The final part, the hardest. Kindnesses come without end, in blue uniforms, and plates of food, held together with a smile. Doctors quietly come and go, leaving morphine as their welcome gift. This is the longest of days.

The love of my life left us at 6am this morning. His body still, his breath gone, and as I looked at him I knew all that was left was this battered shell which housed the most generous, loving, and funny man I had the privilege to know and love. He, the essence of him, was somewhere else.

And so here we will sit. Celebrating a life so fully and seemingly endlessly lived. Legacies of local job clubs, inspirational writing, patient and incisive coaching, rejoicing in others' triumphs when they discover who they really are. And so much more. Peter; father, husband, uncle, brother, cousin, friend, mentor, practical joker, and pun artist. This is my husband, and I will steadfastly refuse to say 'was' because somewhere in the dust, and the breeze, along the white horse waves of the sea, in the flight of the honey bee, there he is. Dust returning to dust, welcomed back to his Mother the Earth, spirit soaring skywards and back, renewed to fly again.

So here we sit. We are broken but he is made whole again.

As I read this diary entry again I am once more so grateful that we had time to say goodbye. That opportunity is not given to us all, but the older I get the more I see there is no 'better' or 'worse' about this business of losing the one you love. No situation is either easier or more difficult in itself. It is always devastating, and we will never have the experience without regrets. But the love we felt, and still feel, shouts out for continued expression. However you choose to do it is up to you. But do it with kindness for yourself and your aching heart.

A Landscape of Grief

3. A different landscape

I am a very visual person. I see things vividly, and perhaps that's why I paint. Pictures drop into my head at random times. Sometimes I think it is God, and at others my own imagination. Perhaps there is little difference between the two, but that's another story. So on this day, very early on in my grieving, I saw a picture of the Menai Strait bridge in my mind. A wonderful piece of graceful architecture, reaching out from the mainland of Wales to land gently on the shores of Anglesey. We visited there as a family when I was small, staying in a low-beamed stone cottage with a leaky roof and uneven floors. Then I seemed to hear the words:

'This is a different landscape. There is no going back.'

A stark metaphor for my current situation. I had joined the ranks of widows and widowers, a term I still hate to this day. With this new and unwelcome status come the questions. Am I still married now? Do I take my wedding rings off? What do I fill out on any form? I know I don't need the answers in this moment but I have to recognise that this landscape I have been forced into is different. There is no going back over that bridge. Nothing can change the truth that Peter has gone.

As we, you and I, take our first footsteps on this foreign ground, we are feeling our way. We can't turn around, only sit and give ourselves time to absorb the reality of where we are. We will feel like walking on sometime, but there is no rush. Take your time. Breathe, and breathe again.

4. Hold your shape

It's a familiar phrase now. Passed on to me by my best friend, spoken to her by a minister's wife. Hold your shape. When all around you is shifting, and nothing seems to make sense, hold your shape by doing all the normal things. Brush your teeth. Comb your hair. Go shopping. Answer the phone, have your meals, do the washing, keep walking, because these mundane things remind us that life goes on, and we cannot stop it no matter how strong our desire or how deep our grief.

And holding your shape also means holding on to who you are. Good friends are the mirror you need. They give you glimpses of happier pasts and possible futures. And they hold onto your bruised and battered hopes when your present is failing. They see footsteps ahead which aren't visible through your own anguish and tears. And the God who sees all, strengthens your tired knees and provides the pathway ahead. All that's left to say is, God is good. In spite of all, God is good. I pray that you can feel a whisper of that truth today.

5. Oh my, but this hurts

Oh my, but this hurts. I see you, Peter, in a cyclist's bright yellow vest as he crosses the road, head down, and rushes for home. I feel you as I walk down the stairs in our favourite place. I stare at you when I see a man with the same wild grey hair. I find you again in the row of your birthday cards left out on the mantelpiece, and I hear your voice echoed in the remembrances of so many friends. I see your hands in the numbers of wooden boxes you assembled for our new pantry. Always keen to keep providing for us your family.

This is so hard. We have crossed a line from which there is no returning, the paths diverge but still we hold hands. And then I see your beautiful portrait on the wall of you painted by Charles Reid, the American artist. And I realise you are still everywhere I go and in everything I see. I cannot escape you, nor do I wish to. Thank God, I still have all this of you.

In these early days we have a terrible and very raw need to connect with our loss, in spite of the pain it causes. This need intrudes as an unbidden guest into our days and nights, but it serves the purpose of remembrance and is mixed with an ongoing flow of tears. There is no need to run from these times. They too will pass. Till then, sit quiet, weep again, and let no one judge you.

A Landscape of Grief

6. A celebration of life

Yesterday was my husband's funeral. We had been both dreading it and wishing it was over, but when it finally arrived it was a beautiful thing. From the slow march of the pallbearer leading the cortège, to the welcome sight of so very many friends outside the church. More like a wedding than a funeral, with over five hundred people wearing something orange, as per Peter's instructions. (Strangely it was also a local election day, and we overheard a passer-by remark that 'Lib-Dem's are out in force today'. Peter would have loved that.)

And there was the hand-decorated coffin, a work of beautiful and original art by my daughter. It cost her greatly to do it in that tiny and silent room at the funeral home, but she knew it was the last thing she could ever give him of herself. One last way for him to be different from the expected. There was an outstanding choir singing from Mozart's requiem, with harmonies that danced and reached the heart, then the quiet of a guitar and the gentlest of love songs. We stood and spoke of our love for a great and extraordinary man who happened to be my husband, the father to my children, and a friend to so very many. People spoke of changed lives, someone talked of Peter living the kingdom of God, and another said, 'He was a man of God, whether he liked it or not'. I liked that. He hated religiosity in any form, and could sniff out a cliché from a mile away.

A Landscape of Grief

They spoke the truth. He couldn't help but be himself, and that, at its core, held an unstoppable drive to help, and a generosity which reached across the world. He changed my life. He was, and is, the love of my life, and I am a better person for having loved him. All we have to do now is figure out how, in this uneasy quietude, to walk the remaining journey without him. There is a void of cosmic magnitude by my side.

A Landscape of Grief

7. This too will pass

This too will pass. Feeling lonely in a crowd. Not being able to finish your sentences because you're so tired. Putting one foot in front of the other, only to be pushed back by the oncoming wind. Whatever it is, it will pass. All things pass. You will feel like smiling one day but it may be slow in coming. Your heart will be lifted by the sight of sun on the water, even if only for a few seconds. Life will be full again, and purpose will return, although never quite the same as before. All has irretrievably changed and we cannot deny that, but like the slow current of a deep and wide river, all you, and I, have to do is allow the current to take us. No need for movement or strain. No use in fighting against the direction of flow. Simply let the river take your weight. Your burdens will feel lighter, and you will be able to see the stars once more. Even if only through your tears.

8. Everything holds a memory

This thing called grief is a strange companion. I don't have a roadmap for this, as my counsellor reminds me, and my mind continues to play tricks on a daily basis. All seems normal as I get on with my day. Then I glance at something, and I remember. I see his shoes by the chair. Empty. I find a pile of his clothes asking to be put away, but I can't move them. I look at the kitchen table and wait for his company. Tears come and go, mixed with a gentle numbness which gets me through the day. But when I look at the sofa, the big orange sofa, I begin to see it as a kaleidoscope of memories. The day we brought it home, it was almost too big for the front door. The years of children playing jumping games on it, hide and seek around it, collapsing exhausted into it, watching cartoons from it. The quiet family evenings falling asleep on it, the Sunday afternoons with cups of tea and the morning paper. The ridiculous number of times the TV remote disappears into its depths, causing everyone to blame the other for its loss.

This is the better side of grief although I can hear you ask, 'Is there any better side?' Perhaps. Perhaps not, but celebrating alongside the raw emotion is all we can do right now. It's all our story. And this newly-shaped absence which I feel as such a gaping reality next to me, is still him. I can only hope it is for you too in your own loss.

A Landscape of Grief

9. The Storm gathers

In the beginning of this unwanted journey, as my suspicions grew that the symptoms Peter was experiencing were more serious than I first thought, I felt the storm clouds gather above us. They were wherever we were, moving with us, some times close, at others following ominously behind us; but regardless of the distance, I always felt that cold whisper in the pit of my stomach. Something is coming. Something is coming.

Just as the clouds on our horizon darkened, so did our world – imperceptibly at first but, as the sky blackened, I realised the wind was taking us in a direction none of us wanted. We had no choice but to go with it.

As someone said, the rain doesn't last forever, and neither does the storm, but if you are still in the middle of your own personal storm, this may be of little comfort to you right now. Whilst we wait for this to pass, all we can do is hold each other close as the storm gathers around us. What will be, will be, but know this; you are not alone. Hold fast.

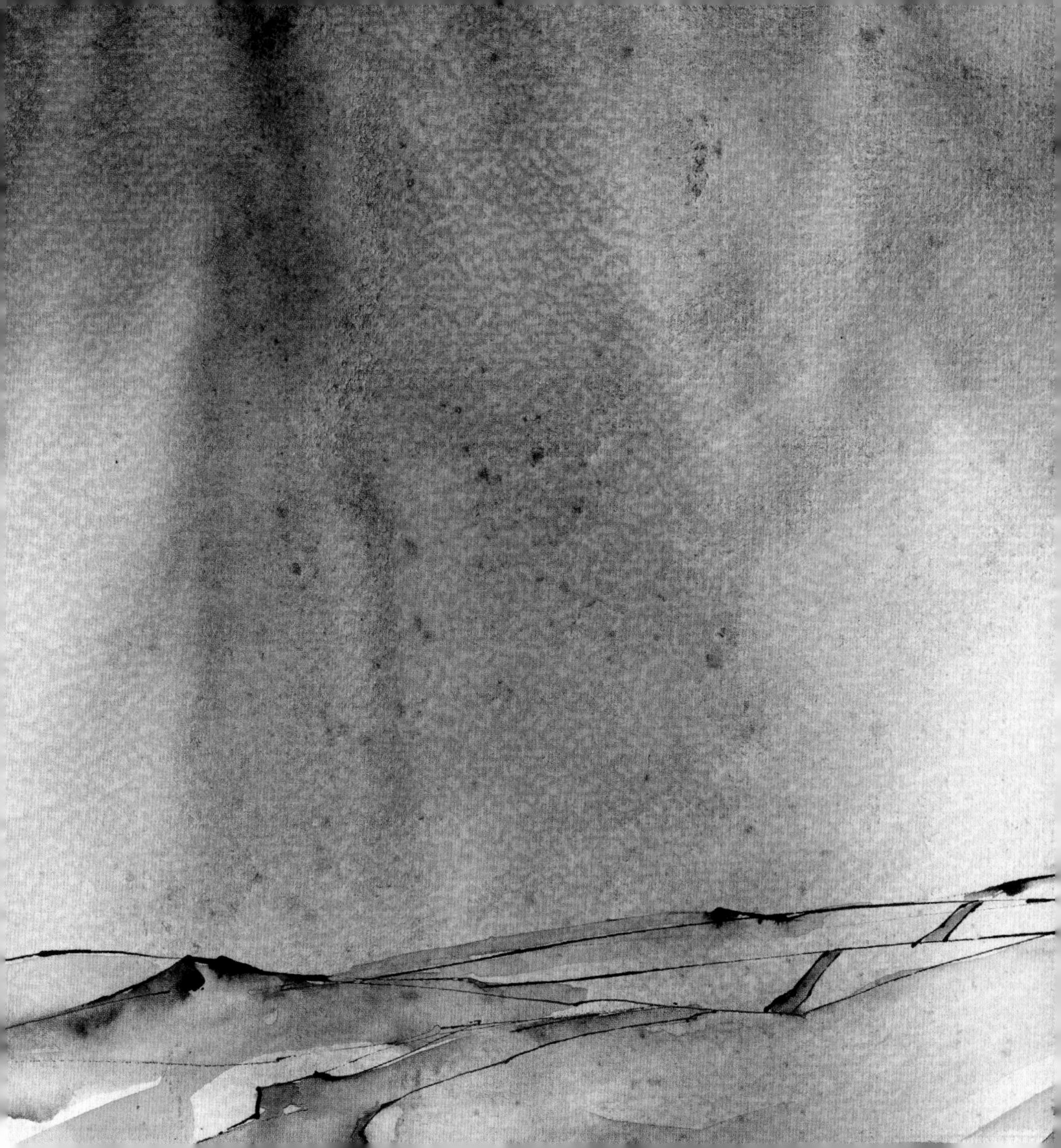

10. Something to hold onto

So there he is. In a green baize box, sitting quietly next to the mantelpiece. My beloved. I collected his ashes from the funeral home yesterday, and what a bizarre experience that was, and continues to be. The weight of him, his physical presence again, contained in the four walls of quiet cardboard. Something for me to hold onto once more, and believe me, I did. Sitting with both arms around him, hugging his solidity, crying in a car park, so blinded by my tears I couldn't drive home. And then the journey home, weaving in and out of the traffic, stops and starts, red lights and green, the normality of it all a stark and painful contrast to the treasure by my side. So now he's home. It's a strange comfort which I didn't expect, to feel that he had returned in some small way. His life in a box that's too small for the enormity of all he was and continues to be.

Life on the outside has returned to some semblance of normal. The dishwasher fills and empties. The hoover runs. The front door opens and closes. The post arrives. The kettle boils. And yet here we are. A deepening void by our side, now partly filled by the quiet green box. Something to hold onto. The house seems to sigh deeply and settle with us now he is home. We will wait awhile, pausing for breath on this next phase of the journey.

And as I sit, I am aware that there is a great company of us who grieve at this moment. We may not know each other but we are still there. Some of us are further along this road than others but that's of no consequence. What matters is that we are not alone. And that is something to hold onto.

A Landscape of Grief

11. Broken Heart Syndrome

It's the pain in my chest that's the worst. Of all the symptoms of grief that I've experienced, it is the most debilitating. A heavy dragging feeling which stops all thought or movement. An ache which is both physical and emotional. A dull thud which changes rhythm from slow and steady to a flutter taking me by surprise with feelings of faint unreality. Am I having a heart attack? Palpitations? No. Apparently I have broken heart syndrome. It is a recognised diagnosis. My life has changed so very radically, from 43 years of knowing and loving and living with Peter to suddenly being catapulted into a different and very empty world. The space at my side is both a presence and an absence, a hole of immense depth which at any moment I think I might fall into. I wish for him but know I cannot have him. I speak his name but I know he cannot answer. There is only the reminder of this unprecedented silence, now part of my life. Perhaps one day it will become familiar to me rather than this terrible aching loss by my side.

Strangely the recognition of this pain, this broken heart which is common to all who grieve, is the oddest of comforts. We are not failing, just hurting. We do not need 'fixing', just understanding. We cannot rush this thing called grief but surrender ourselves to it, trusting that as Mother Julian of Norwich said, all will be well. In the end.

12. Empty hands

Every day I look for his hand to hold when I walk. I reach for him in the sleepy first light, and at the embers of each dying day. I search for him on the hills. I feel his shadow behind me but my hands remain empty. Always empty. Regardless of my feverish activity or painful stillness, my hands are empty. I know I will carry this emptiness for the rest of my living, always there, searing my heart with its ever-present reality. I am told it will change, that I will adjust, that this burden may feel lighter in time, but there is no real change in the rawness of the pain. It is as it is. He is gone. And I am here.

Grief rips away all that we take for granted, leaving only emptiness. We didn't want to ever imagine life without them but now we are forced to. So what can we do except continue to look for reasons to keep on breathing. We have more life to live and that is a gift not granted to all. There's no reasoning as to why him, and why me. These questions, to my mind, only cause more frustration, even pain. I have to hold to the mystery of God and the ongoing mystery of life as it unfolds before me. My hope is that today you too, wherever you are and however you are feeling, can trust your empty hands to the peace inside you. They will be full again someday. In the meantime, we will wait together.

13. He was my comfort blanket

I woke up feeling panic this morning. Tightness across my chest, breath coming too quickly. I walked into the early sun to escape it but it kept coming after me. A new companion, this anxiety, and it seems I can't run from it. I have to face it, allow it, and wait for it to pass. Peter was always there regardless of the view ahead or the road behind. My companion in all we did. I never fully realised how close we were even when separated by physical distance. I referred my actions and plans to the map of life he held for us both, and he lived, as I now see, to be a help to us all. Now I must write on this stark white page, this map which has no road. God help me.

I wonder if the best thing to do when we feel anxious is to simply accept it. I find this extremely difficult, as I immediately look for an escape route. To run from the feelings, the tightness, the aching, the sleeplessness, the whirling mind. But I've learnt to my cost that this way of reacting doesn't work. Not for long. So these days I reach for someone to talk to. Family, a friend, my therapist. And I slow down. And breathe.

Our bodies will signal our distress to us over and over again until we stop and listen. And then, when we listen with enough love for ourselves, we can turn our running into gentle and healing self-care. So sit down, take a breath or two, and listen. You will hear what you need. Go gently through these next few days. And remember you are loved.

14. A visible sign of mourning

It was once the custom to wear black if you were in mourning. A sign for the community to acknowledge your pain. Or later, an armband of black linen. A signal that your world has collapsed. I find myself wanting to wear black. I need to let the world around me know of our grief. No details but just a quiet sign to be gentle with us as a family. I'm standing in the supermarket crying in front of the bread aisle and then losing my way amongst the baked bean tins, unable to make a decision. I need to warn you, if you're passing by, of the rage and pain inside. It's not aimed at you but it explains why I am like I am. I cannot understand how this world can carry on without marking this enormous loss. Your world is the same as it was when you woke up this morning, and most other mornings, or at least it appears that way to me. I woke this morning and remembered. I need to speak his name to the air, to bring him back to life for just one moment. I want to shout his loss to the sky and tell the world to stop turning. I long to tell you of the great man he was, the way he smiled, the sound of his laugh. Of his unending generosity if you needed help. He'd find your potential and point you to the life you hoped for when you doubted you might deserve it. And yes, like everybody, Peter wasn't perfect, but he'd always cheer for your small victories, and celebrate your determination. His loss has left a terrible absence.

As a society we shy away from those who are grieving. We step away respectfully because we don't know what to say and I suspect we don't talk of death because we want to pretend it won't happen to us. But it does and I wonder if we need a more obvious display of our mourning. So if you feel the same as I do, wear black. Talk about your loved one whenever, wherever you can. Cry without embarrassment or apology. And forgive the world over and over for not knowing about your pain.

15. I don't argue with the process

When my mother died, my father took up his pen as usual. He journalled throughout his life and I never understood why until I began myself. Writing becomes an audible expression of ourselves within the reader, but also it's somewhere to voice our thoughts and hopes. Dad wrote this poem shortly after his loss.

Question

I don't argue with the process –
birth, life, and death –
the orderly progression
to death's inevitability.
I simply question the pain.
The pain of loss.
A God of love, you say
and yet the more one loves
the greater is the hurt
at parting.
Birth's pain is soon forgotten
in new life's joy
but there is little comfort
in the losing
and pious words, well meant,
just fall on stony ground
and wither.

Time heals, I'm told
but each day's dawn
repeats the grief.
The open wound
rubbed raw still bleeds.
And holding on to faith
asks almost more than
I can give.
Lord, I believe, but only just.
Yesterday's promises
taste stale.
All I can offer is what I am,
you'll have to be content
with that.

After Peter died, I read this poem again. I have to agree with Dad, we cannot argue about the seasons of life but my heart breaks with the brutality of what I see and what we experience. The progress of his illness, the suffering, the slow deterioration, unbearable to watch in someone you love. All we can do is be honest as to how we feel, and stand with our loved ones as long as we are able. Love is all we have, after all.

16. If loving was enough

In the early days after my father died, I realised that deep down, just for a moment, I believed if I cried enough, longed enough, even loved enough, God would bring him back. An old memory perhaps from childhood when a parent can make things right with a simple kiss or a hug. Those years do not last and the harsh reality is that loss and joy travel together with us, each showing their face to us turn by turn.

I wrote this poem after my father died. It's written from the perspective of Joseph of Arimathea, as he prepares the body of Jesus together with Nicodemus, both disciples of Jesus in their own way.

'This cannot be', my heart despairs,
as I cradle his body now,
he who showed me life itself,
healed with one touch,
and delivered from death with one word,
he who lies life-less now.

Holding his hand in mine,
the cold bites into my heart,
etching it with pain,
covering it with darkness.

A Landscape of Grief

'This cannot be' – our tears, my brother's and mine,
fall freely on his face.
If longing could bring him back,
he would be ours once more

And as we lay him down, my Dearest Friend,
surrounded by the damp of earth and stone,
he lies peaceful now, beyond us,
we remember what we once dared hope for,
that this is not the end.
This cannot, should not, will not, be the end.

If loving was enough, there would be no loss, no separation through death but nothing I can do will bring my father, or my husband, back to me. But, and I do believe this with every weary fibre of my being, that death is not the end of life. Somehow, somewhere, we go on.

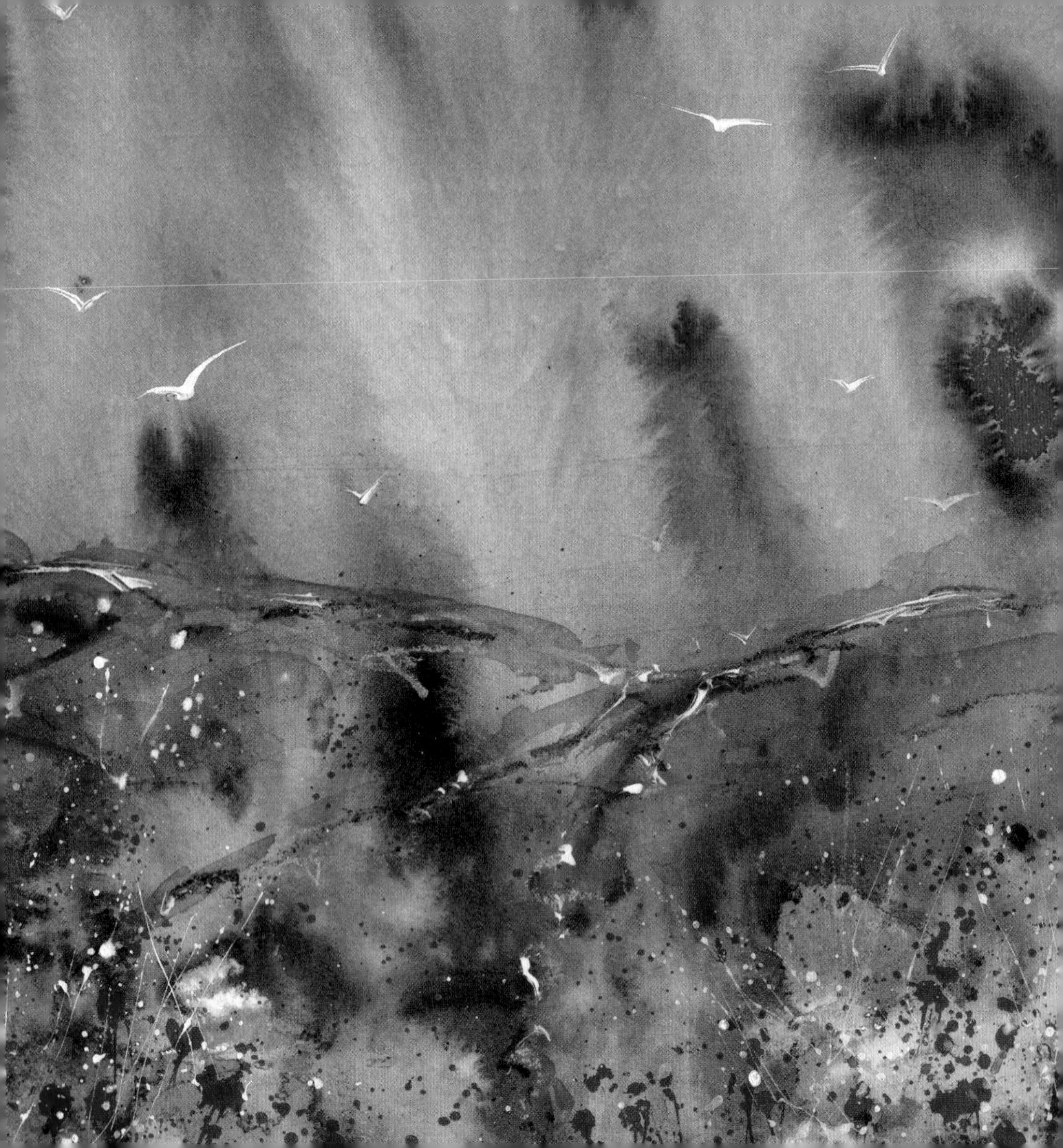

17. The guilt of laughter

There comes a day when you will laugh, and you will catch yourself and stop because it feels so wrong. Laughing is linked to joy, and since your loss, you cannot feel any other emotion except grief. So when laughter breaks in, it shakes you to the core, as if there is an unwritten rule that says you cannot smile again. Guilt floods in, stifling the momentary lightness of spirit and returning you to the more familiar sadness.

But life is full of contrasts, or at least it should be, and when joy arrives, like the echo of a distant trumpet, it calls us to the present moment where laughter has returned. Joy will come again, as will the tears, and the heartache, and the confusion. So be assured, joy will show itself, and we will learn to rest in it again.

18. We haven't had that conversation yet

We haven't had that conversation yet, God. One day we will. We haven't talked about why, and how it seemed that you turned away, leaving a void of well-meant platitudes, and a sudden and overwhelming sadness. We haven't talked about why you say we can, and should, see healing when we pray, and yet so much has not yet happened. For so many.

I haven't voiced my enveloping pain at how Peter was robbed of more good life to come. Twenty years by his reckoning. And how his children, our children, have had their hearts broken, over and over, inch by inch, during the last two years. We have never talked of the burning anger, and the deepest sadness which rolls over us all, family and friends, with now monotonous regularity.

But, and here it comes, as the song says ('I can't get enough of your amazing love' by Leeland), 'I can't walk away. No, I can't walk away. For I have seen your face so I can't walk away'. Perhaps this, at its deepest level, is what faith looks like. The knowing and the not-knowing. The latter is building as quickly as the former is shrinking. As for that conversation, it can wait a while longer. I have a suspicion that God knows all of this already but the answers I'm wanting right now may never come. Hopefully you and I can learn to accept that. Answers won't bring our loved ones back. And the most courageous thing that you and I can do right now is to still believe, and not walk away. Hold on to that ever-moving thing called faith, resist the temptation to explain it, even justify it. Just hold it lightly, with grace and love.

19. The language of grief, and what not to say

Sorrow, anguish, weeping, disbelief, rage, numbness, paralysis, longing. The spectrum of words to describe the feelings and reactions we experience in response to enormous loss is infinite.

In the very early days of our grief, there were so many moments where we held our fragility with numb hands, and words spoken by others sounded hollow, like the beating of an old and damaged drum. The perception and understanding of ordinary language now felt like the strangest of ancient dialects. Meaning escaped us through the air as fast as the words were spoken. All done with good intent, but it was all too soon.

As humans we seem to need to fill the space between one breath and another. Silence feels like a threat to our security, and so often people talked to us with an uncomfortable and sometimes erratic energy, as if trying to force us to feel better in response to their brief offerings of comfort.

I have been shocked and hurt, and if I'm totally honest, deeply disheartened by the things people said at first when confronted with our pain. They were all well-meaning, or at least I have to believe so, otherwise bitterness might creep in to add to the pain of loss, giving it an extra barb to catch me on. So, hoping to avoid this sort of pain for others, here are some of the most often repeated things that you, dear reader, might want to avoid.

> 'You'll get over it.'
> 'It was his time.'
> 'I know how you feel, my friend/sister/cousin died of it last year.'
> 'It was to bring God glory.'
> 'It's God's will.'
> 'You'll see him again, and won't that be wonderful!'
> 'Are you still grieving?'

If I were to believe any or all of these responses it would mean that my God is a vindictive God who sent us, or allowed, this terrible suffering in order to accomplish some heavenly purpose, but I am convinced more with each day God does not. We malign that Holy Presence with intentions and actions which were never there.

Words spoken, however kindly meant, can never be taken back, and therein lies a pool of sadness and regret we have all experienced at some time in our lives. We never mean to hurt one another, but I wonder why we feel we need to fill that space with words if someone is grieving. For me it has often felt like someone is stepping over my pain in order to drag me with them. Grief is always hard to watch in others, but it is something we must learn to walk alongside, in silence if we need to.

There is no time limit to grief. One of my present favourite phrases is 'It is as it is'. How you feel right now, whether you are weeping or sitting with a creeping numbness in your heart, it's okay. That's where you are today, or as my wonderful friend says, 'This is the emotion for today'. You do not need 'fixing'. All the therapy I have had has taught me not to run from the pain, the heartbreak, the confusion, even the transient and guilt-ridden laughter. This, what is in your heart

now, is enough for today. Words have great power, to heal, to capture imagination and portray the deepest of feelings when we have no words ourselves.

I guess the moral of the story is, think carefully, speak gently, and hold fast to those you love. And if you are hurting from the memories of words spoken to you, take a breath. They meant no harm, and you need no more heaviness to add to the burden you carry. Let go, as they say, and let God.

A Landscape of Grief

20. Single-minded

There is a plant in my garden which I particularly love. It's the purple verbena, which has clusters of the tiniest purple flowers erupting from the most slender of stems. These stems each grow to about three feet or more but are much thinner than my little finger. It makes me wonder how they can remain upright and so strong in the face of the winds and rains of summer. After some brief research online, the anatomy of the plant, which seems incredibly complex at a microscopic level, is basically a hollow tube in a quadrilateral shape. A simple design. And with an even simpler purpose: to quietly and single-mindedly grow, support, and feed these minute flowers. Again and again. That's all.

Some of us know that single-mindedness from an early age. We know what we are meant for. Others of us take a lifetime to know it. Either way is fine, we will know who we are. And who we are and what we are meant for remains, regardless of what we are going through. Storms come and go, but when grief hits, we can all too quickly lose all sense of who we are. We will find that sense again. In time. Till then we need to stay connected to whatever or whoever supports us. Just like the stems of the purple verbena. So hold fast. You are who you are. You are not lost.

A Landscape of Grief

21. Faith stripped bare

Faith is a strange thing. We spend our early years being told, gently or more firmly, who God is and how we should relate to him. We hear the ancient stories and the meanings which generations of our elders have attributed to each and every nuance. We are encouraged to accept that this is how things are. Here are the rules, however subtle or blatant. In my experience every church, and I think every faith, has its rules. And because we want to do the right thing and align ourselves with all that is good and all that is loving, we live the best way we can within these expectations. And that's mostly to the good. But there will come a time in our lives, which in Richard Rohr's book *Falling Upwards*, is described as a letting go of all that we thought we knew in order to find ourselves more fully, and to find God again. Going on takes courage, and as someone said recently, 'Courage takes courage.'

Born into a missionary family, I never knew a time without a sense of God. Weekly prayer meetings in the lounge with the other missionaries, as a child, I used to beg Dad to let me sit with them in the quiet which settled around us all like an invisible blanket. All they did was based on the deepest values of love and compassion, and when we came back to England the traditions of church and all that meant carried on. Baptist, Church of England, House Church, Vineyard – over the years I loved them all in their way, and early in our marriage Peter and I immersed ourselves in running youth groups wherever we were. We had our own troubles – I experienced years of chronic pain and other hardships – but nothing really shook my faith until Peter was diagnosed with Motor Neurone Disease. I suspect it began when I noticed the first worrying signs. The fear of what was to come. And the desperate prayers. Over the two years, we prayed. We begged. We despaired. We hoped. We believed. And nothing. No healing. No halt to the changes. No promises fulfilled. But strangely that wasn't what really shook me. In the beginning, it was the desperate loneliness of walking this road with so few coming with us. And after he was gone, I felt had to look more closely at this God of mine, and the doctrines and traditions I had been brought up in. Being in church felt like being in an alien place. I no longer understood the language spoken, and my heart was too heavy to give voice to any song. All the scaffolding of my faith had fallen to the cold, hard ground. Forced to look for what was left, I walked away, not from God but from the building and all that it signified, and out into the open air. And I found new joy in the song of the wren. The whisper of His presence in the night sky.

Comfort in the rhythm of the waves. It was a different way of being.

I realised that if I had the courage to let my accepted theology go, and to welcome every question I faced as a friend rather than a failure, I might find God was still there in all Her glory. And I don't say 'Her' lightly. It's because I have experienced more of the feminine love and compassion of God in these few years than in all the years before. God is.

Theology, traditional or otherwise, is a book we are rewriting as the centuries progress. A book to be handled with respect, love, and care, but it is not a rule book which cannot be touched because of fear. When the scaffolding comes away, when all the props to our faith are removed, we have to have the courage to explore what is left.

And there is my miracle. When all was stripped bare, there was God. At the core of my faith I have lost nothing. In truth I have found a depth of love and self-awareness I am so grateful for. God is mystery. God is joy. God is.

22. Teach us to lament

We are not taught to lament. Brought up on stories of victory, of triumph over troubles, of God stepping in to rescue us, of so many answers to prayer, so we are taught to rejoice. Some churches I have experienced leant more towards an expectation of healing through prayer, but few churches taught us how to carry on when healing never came. You just kept going forwards for more prayer. And more. And on many levels, there is nothing wrong with that. We are told to keep praying. But in the face of ongoing sickness or pain we need a different model to show us what to say when there is no answer, when there is nothing but silence, and our prayers are lost in the vacuum of our spoken words. We need to find the voice of true lament. I found mine in the words I wrote below.

Lament

Rudderless on unknown seas
I sit bereft
His empty seat beside me,
A chasm of immeasurable depth.
The compass needle swings as caught by a whirlpool
And I am lost

Ragged breaths offset by tears because he is gone,
he is gone
he is gone
And I am left.

There is no precedent for grief,
No map, no charted course.
It is enough to hold on,
gripping the boat.
No point to the oars.
There is no direction to be found.
Only the pain of waiting, hoping, weeping.
I am lost.

Lament is a form of deepest sorrow. It does not mean we are losing our faith although it may feel like that. It is simply a raw and honest emotion expressing the anguish we feel. We need to have a safe place in which to give voice to our anguish. Lament recognises that we are powerless in the face of what has happened, and there are no words adequate to help or to lighten our loss. It is what we need, whether a silent positioning with others close to us, or a deep groan of emotion. Lament is wordless, and it lasts for as long as it lasts.

I have to admit I have always had great difficulty with the complex story of Job, but what I have found immensely valuable is the poignant picture of Job's friends gathering round him in his loss, sitting with him for seven days.

> 'Then they sat on the ground with him for seven days and nights. No one said a word to Job, for they saw that his suffering was too great for words'.
>
> Job 2:13 (New Living Translation)

Nothing more. No words were spoken. No platitudes. No wisdom or reasons for his tragedy. I picture them crouching with him in the dust, embarrassed at first as the silence envelops them all, but then slowly settling into the reality that they could do nothing more than just sit. That is perhaps one of the greatest gifts I have been given by my family and few remaining friends through these times. They chose to sit with me, and they sit with me still. Over and over. Quietly holding my hand. And I am so grateful they do not fill the air with phrases well-worn over so many decades, which are designed to help but in reality do little else but sting like a biting north wind.

Sit in the dust with me whilst together we sing our song of lament.

A Landscape of Grief

23. Time enough

Yesterday my daughter noticed I hadn't been wearing my watch recently. Probably because I kept asking her what the time was. She asked why I had stopped wearing it, which made me think more deeply than normal. Why had I stopped wearing it? Because – and this realisation came out of nowhere – it was my unconscious protest against time carrying on when everything in me wanted it to stop since Peter died. My world had been brought to a complete and terrifying halt by an earthquake of cataclysmic proportions. How can the rest of the world keep on moving? And yet it did, and still does.

It's the same for all of us. My sister pointed out recently that there are people all around us carrying their own silent heartbreak which we may never know about. But that is the way of things. The world still turns, the sun still sets and rises, and hopes and fears come and go. What else can we do except carry on living, breathing in God's good air and feeling the sun on our faces when it comes? There's time enough for joy to return. So, in the meantime, we'll sit quiet, and wait a while longer.

24. Marking time

Feeling low a few days ago, I was talking with my sister about how I felt. I realised that since Peter's death I feel like I'm just waiting. Waiting most days, for something meaningful to do? For a feeling of peace to come? Or in truth, I'm waiting for him to come home. My sister commented:

'You're marking time. That's what waiting is.'

That hit home. Marking time, as per the definition she later shared, is a military step in which soldiers march in place, moving their legs as in marching rhythm, but without ever stepping forward. It's staying in the same place without any change in direction. Motion without progress. So that's where I am, and probably some of you too. No point pushing forwards or backwards. No sense in going to the right or the left for we cannot sidestep this thing that has happened to us. And why would we want to move? We need to find a place of acceptance, and because life has changed so radically for us, we need time. Time to think, to process, to regroup, and to stay in one place whilst we heal. And that, my friends, may take a long time. So let's accept that marking time, for now, is what we are supposed to do.

25. Strong therapy

So I'm on my normal morning walk and I pass the pub which always has four or five beautiful hanging baskets suspended high on its walls throughout the summer. There is deep blue and purple lobelias, scarlet begonias, and snow-white geraniums, and, for once, I was early enough to see the man who waters them each day. I noticed he had put feed into the water this time so I asked if he fed the plants every day. He said, no, just once a week but today was different because of the storms. He then added:

'If you'd been battered by gale force winds of 90 miles an hour, you'd need strong therapy.'

So there he was, feeding and watering the most affected ones, encouraging them back to life. He said it might take a week or so, but they would recover. Food and water from someone who knows. And I realise that this story has a wider reach. I've suffered recent storm damage, as have most of us. And what we need now is strong therapy. Food, water, and ongoing care. Even if we feel we may never fully recover, we will be brought back to life eventually. There is something to be said in recognising when we need help. I'm not sure I could've survived as I have without seeing my therapist over the last many months. So drink up, eat up, ask for help when you need it, and rest while you wait.

A Landscape of Grief

26. Is it okay if I say ...?

I've been thinking lately about honesty. Not the regular sort of honesty of trying not to tell lies or deceive anyone, but more about what we buy into. And by that I mean beliefs, and church, and faith, and religion. Lately I've been thinking how it might be if there was a gathering, which we might one day call church, and it will be a place where we can interrupt the preacher or the singer, and say:

'Can you tell me, do you really believe what you've been saying? Can we talk about the words we've just been singing, and what that really means?'

Because as I see it now, church is far from a place like that.

We sang a song in church a few weeks back. The words go something like this: 'I cry out for your hand of mercy to heal me ...'

And it hit me that I couldn't in all honesty sing that anymore. Because if I did it would mean I believe that I have to cry and beg my god for healing. And if he doesn't heal me that means he wasn't merciful to me. And if he's not merciful, then what does that say about his character? And his love?

I didn't interrupt the song. Because it's not the sort of thing one does in a church. Yet. And since then there have been countless more times when I've wanted to shout out, hang on, do you really believe what you are saying? Have you really thought about this?

A Landscape of Grief

I need a place where I can feel okay if I say I'm struggling to believe all that I once did. And where it's okay if I admit to losing my grip on what I thought faith was, whilst at the same time finding something new that I can't quite hold in my hands because it's too big and unknowable. I think it's Love. And the mystery of God.

And is it okay if I say what I really feel about the Bible, and feminism, and the way women have suffered for millennia just for being women?

And will I still have a place here if I say I can't believe all that you do? And so much more? Maybe, maybe not – I've experienced both.

So that's my dream. One day, one glorious day, we will all be welcomed. You and I, with our arms full of doubts, sadness, and questions, holding on to a faith which looks unrecognisable to most. And in that place we will be drawn in with open arms, generous hearts, and time enough to hear each other in an atmosphere of love. And without the demand for us to change.

One day. One glorious day.

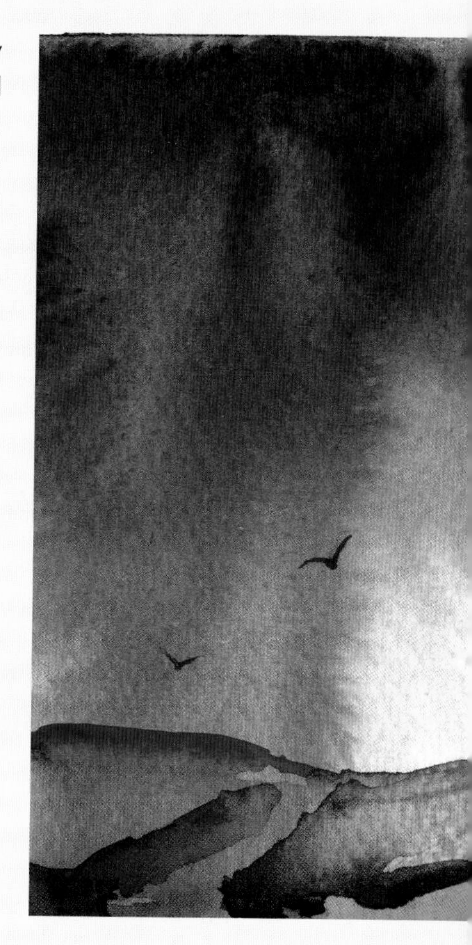

27. When time stands still by the door

It's been eight painfully long months since Peter died. I cannot put into words what that has meant for us as a family. The enormity of this loss is too raw. But then I remembered the book *Walking into the Light: A Journey through Grief*, which I put together using the poems and thoughts my dad wrote when mum died. Writing parts of it helped my sister and I to grieve. I thought of the penultimate paragraph I wrote.

Read on.

> If you are grieving, there will be times when you wake, and all seems normal. The day fills, and the sadness of your loss lies light across your shoulders.
>
> And yet there will be days, when no matter how strong the intention, another wave of grief will come, pressing down, taking your breath away. It will take your attention again, and you will pause, and listen, and weep, and wait for it to pass. These are the days where kindness is needed, where expectations must stay soft amongst the bedclothes as memories beckon, and time stands still by the door. We pause and wait for these days to pass in a

bittersweet haze, mystified at the passage of the world without us.
We wait, until Hope appears at the door.

There is little more to be said today. If you have lost someone too, somehow we walk this road together. If you have suffered no loss then look at us with kindness and look with gratitude at your life.

28. One glorious continuum

New Year's Day, and I admit to having dreaded it this year. Another new year without you. Months stretched out by each individual hour. Seconds tick and there is no change. You are still not here. Absence is so much deeper than I imagined. It hangs in the air like morning mist but never fully evaporates, even in the heat of day. My reasons are obvious but I have also been wondering why we seem to make the idea of a New Year so special. Perhaps it stems from a need to hope in the future, to acknowledge past joys, and to break away from personal regrets. But as one day fades and another day dawns it occurs to me that there is no break in this. The river flows and never stops. The stream which feeds it does not segment itself into neat little parcels from one year to the next. It is all one. Everything leads to the sea. Everything we are and everything of worth that we have ever done, comes with us in one glorious continuum. Today is no different from any other. Just another day weighed and measured for us to fill with all the good we can do and all the joy we can experience. Let this day be as it is for you. Take it as a gift, like every day. Breathe it into your life as only you are able, and leave space for others to fill.

A Landscape of Grief

29. Here it comes again

Another wave. Nausea, palpable anxiety, and a level of static in the air as the thunderclouds of grief roll in. And I am overwhelmed. Again. I look around my room for something to hold onto. His pillow, which still lies on his side of the bed. His glasses on the bedside table. But those are of a gossamer-thin comfort, dissolving into the air as my reality throws me off course again. I should be accustomed to this by now. Thirteen months and counting but his last week is still as close to me as my own breath. A whirlwind of memory threatens but I must turn away just for now. There's enough to do in the business of living through this next moment. Enough just to take the next breath. And the next. And the next.

I wonder sometimes if we are too hard on ourselves, as well as each other. There is no rule book on how to grieve, and no timetable as to when we should be able to face the rest of our lives. So we need not be surprised by the rolling waves of emotion which simply keep on coming. And as my therapist says, don't run from it. This feeling is the feeling for today. It will pass, so hold tight. It will pass. And, as I always want to believe, we are not alone.

30. On the edge of the world

This thing called grief is the strangest thing. It throws you into free fall. I thought today how easy it would be to believe that the world was indeed flat, as these days it feels like I have fallen off the very edge. It just seems that the normal rules of gravity, or the return of sunrise and sunset, the beginnings and ends to the seasons – none of them make any sense anymore. Or perhaps it just feels right now that little of it matters. It is as if you are suspended in space watching the world in its own orbit from a truly terrifying height.

This is not written for a sympathy vote. It's just an observation of the most unsettled time of life I have ever been through. But then I am gently surprised and gifted by the conversations of friends today, who remind me that I am still a part of this life of ours. In the words of William Wordsworth, 'our minds are nourished and invisibly repaired' by such normal conversations. I am blessed by such friends.

All I can hope for is that you too, as you read this, holding on as you are to this life in the midst of all your confusion, will find such conversations, as I have, to remind you of who you are, and that you are precious, and always have been.

A Landscape of Grief

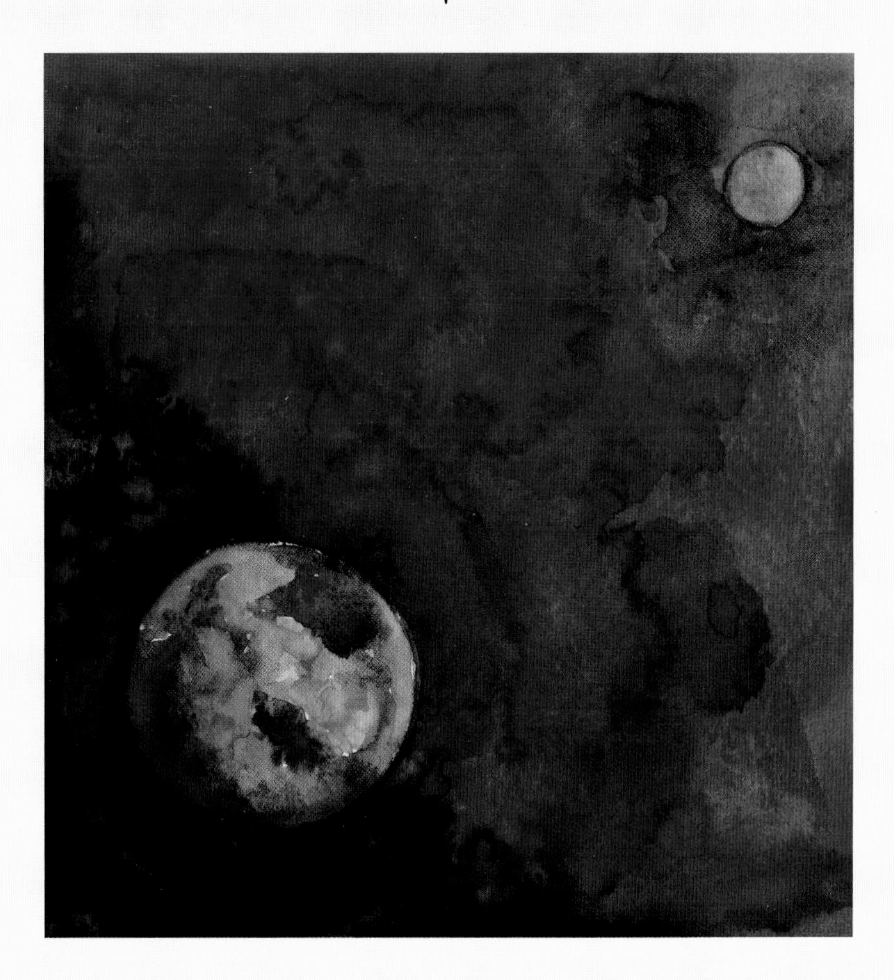

31. Let there be no waste in life

I've been collecting the last of the rose hips from my garden so that I'll have enough rose hip syrup for the winter this year. Apparently it's got much more vitamin C than ordinary oranges so last year I made it for the first time. Pick your rose hips, top and tail them, wash them and then pour them into Kilner jars. Cover them completely with as much sugar as you can pack in, put the lid on and then wait for the magic to happen. In a few weeks' time you'll have some beautiful golden syrup to boost your immune system.

So whilst I was topping and tailing my rose hips I thought how wonderful nature is. Everything valued and everything used. Eaten by the birds or collected by us. I wonder if there is a parallel in life. Perhaps not in every situation. I don't think I'll ever see any good come out of what Peter went through, but I can believe that God can make good out of bad. Sometimes. Our experiences shape us, make us who we are, and if that makes us more able to help people in similar situations, then that to me is showing that, for a brief and beautiful moment, there is no waste in life. Like my rose hip syrup, we can sweeten the taste of life for those around us.

A Landscape of Grief

32. Playing the death card

Peter always had a wicked and very dry sense of humour and during his illness there were moments when it would re-emerge with a freshness that surprised us all. When we put our offer in for the cottage in Dorset we were told it would take six to eight weeks before we could move in. Peter looked at me with a smile and said, 'You could always play the death card!' I was slightly taken aback but I knew why he was saying it. We might as well get some minuscule advantage through facing this horrible disease. I mentioned our situation to the estate agents through my tears, and we were able to move in within two and a half weeks. It can be done, and all because of their amazing kindnesses. There were other times when we used the death card again, and in the early days it always made Peter look slightly smug. A little joy in extremis.

It is strange how humour comes to us in the midst of grief. There is a fleeting relief with the surprise of our own laughter, however momentary that might be. Smiling may feel quite alien for some time to come but little by little it will feel more like a normal response to parts of our day. And remember, laughter leads to hope, and hope to joy. And joy is a reminder that we who are still here can live and love and weep and laugh in equal measure.

33. At least we had time

Death at any time is a shock for those left behind. Hard to grasp that the person who occupied that space beside you is no longer there, but I can't help feeling grateful in a strange way that we had ample warning. I feel for those whose loved one left so suddenly that their last breath lingered in the air before the loss was fully understood. We had two years which were both a torture and a joy in mixed quantities. We could face the truth and run from it in turns, time and time again, as we decided how the remaining months would be. Spring turned into a tenuous summer as we enjoyed the sea breezes on the coast fulfilling a long-held dream that had gained an understandable urgency. The diagnosis was always there but we became experts at ignoring the changes until they became so stark we couldn't climb over them. Time began to speed up as the symptoms in Peter multiplied, and suddenly we were nearing the final stretch. But I am still grateful for the time we had. Preparation was everything to Peter, so he had time to organise his leaving, and we had time to treasure him.

But as I reflect on how this might seem to you, whatever your situation and your experience, I am coming to the conclusion there is never enough time, and no one situation is any easier or more difficult than any other. I cannot measure my pain against yours. It is as it is. We have a loss that will be with us for the rest of our days.

A Landscape of Grief

I sometimes hear people say, 'I would give anything to have just one more hug, to hear his or her voice again', but for me I realised early on that one more hug would never be enough. I would always want more. Hearing his voice again might be a temporary comfort but when it has disappeared again, we are still left as we were. Separated. So I turn away from these longings with whatever small strength I might find in that moment, and doggedly get on with my day. We can change nothing in our past, so step away with me and find yourself some momentary peace.

34. There will always be regrets

I have learned that there will always be regrets so I'm no longer surprised by the pain of them when they come. They are an unwelcome additional part of grief and I believe that even if you were able to say all you could to your loved one, that you gave every possible kindness at the time, that you were as prepared as much as you could be, regrets will still creep in by stealth with a voice that's hard to ignore. Whispers of how you missed something, of why didn't you notice this or that, will bombard you when you least expect it. Or for me, the fact that the normal irritations of life seemed at times to amplify and I showed my frustration. And so did he. Looking back, these regrets are still very raw. It's strange to admit it now but I had this naive idea that once the diagnosis was given I would transform into this endlessly patient, endlessly loving, endlessly forgiving wife. In short, I would become pretty

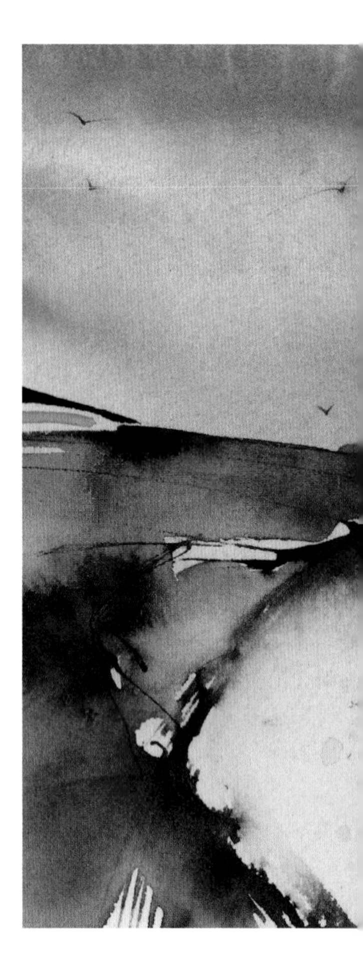

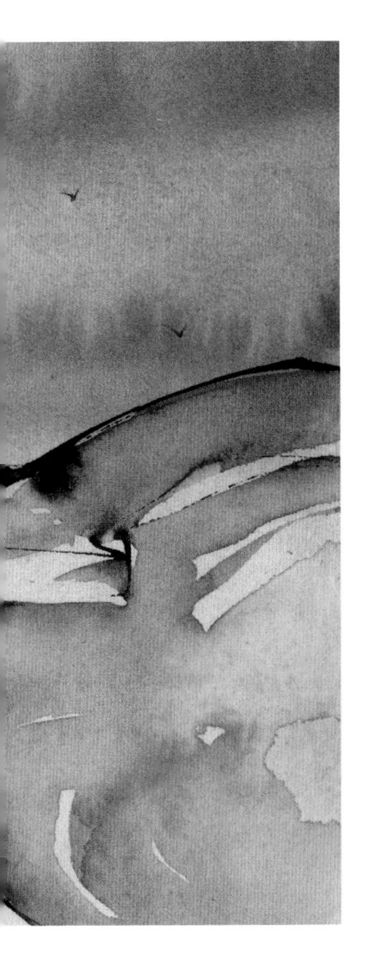

much perfect in the face of a terminal illness. Sad to say, I didn't. I think I did okay, and Peter told others I was wonderful but this didn't protect me from looking back and wishing I had been kinder every day. A small consolation to hold onto if you are in the midst of these unpredictable seas, is that, like riding a wave, these thoughts will eventually pass you by, and you will survive. The voices fade in time although some may lodge deep within you but you will get accustomed to their presence and give them no notice. They will take less and less space in your heart, having found a shady corner, like a forgotten piece of furniture, to hide in. Accept they are there, and when they show themselves, accept yourself for getting momentarily drawn in. Wait patiently for the thoughts to pass. And in all this, practice the gentle art of forgiving yourself, and loving yourself. You are doing the best you can with the resources you have right now, just as you did then. And you are now part of a community of men and women who are walking this same land, perhaps with different circumstances but all with grief as their companion.

35. Holding on to the material

When my mum died I made jam. I realised months later that it seemed to me to be a way of keeping some small sense of control. After weeks of filling my small glass jars I stopped to reflect, and wrote this poem.

When she died, I made jam.
Took comfort in the steady movement.
The chopping, peeling, slicing.
Slow roll of the darkening fruit.
Steam rising in my orange kitchen,
a gentle mix for my tears.

The jam jars stand
nudging shoulders quietly on the shelf,
a promise of sweetness to come.
The tight covers stretch with loving tension
as I hold my breath
waiting to begin again

A Landscape of Grief

When my father died, just over six months later, I found myself unable to let go of the tiniest scraps of paper which had his handwriting on. It felt to me a betrayal, a throwing away of small parts of him, over and over. I still find it hard even now, and this feeling has amplified now Peter has gone.

I believe these reactions are normal. So if someone urges you to let go of any item, or to change the way you are grieving, please very gently ignore them. Unless of course what you are doing is proving a harm to yourself or anyone else. We do the best we can. Peter would tell me that over and over, when I was discouraged or ashamed over past behaviour: we do the best we can. So if you still need to hold onto your loved one's clothes, or handwriting, or text messages, that's okay. Believe me. You are doing okay. So go gently through this day, especially if it is particularly hard in this moment.

36. This is holy ground

It's eighteen months as I write this. The seasons move on regardless of how we feel or what we do to try to stop them, and with each day that passes I have a growing suspicion that we walk on holy ground. Not as Moses and the burning bush, if you are familiar with the tale of God's encounter with a broken man and a bush of flames, but because the harshness of life opens up a way for the divine. Moments when you know, you know, you know, without a doubt, that something Other is there with you. The essence of all things created breathes on you. Just for a second. And that moment has to sustain you for all the darkness of the next moment. Like the sun piercing through the thunderclouds overhead. And no, I'm not promising silver linings, as there are none to be had here. Just an awareness that Mother Julian perhaps knew more than I do when she said:

'All will be well, and all will be well, and all manner of thing will be well'.

In the end, all may indeed be well. Not now. Not tomorrow. But sometime in the future when all things are as they should be, all will be well.

I sometimes dream I am flying. Able to swoop low to the ground and then I am lifted up to a joyous height. In my dream there is no fear, no limit to my movement, no hurry to be anywhere. Just joy. Pure and simple. This too is the experience of holy ground. That moment where nothing else matters except to enjoy life as it was meant to be. Do not doubt that this will happen for you too. It may come in the whisper of a dream or as a moment so light you doubt your experience, but come it will. The reminder that you too walk on holy ground.

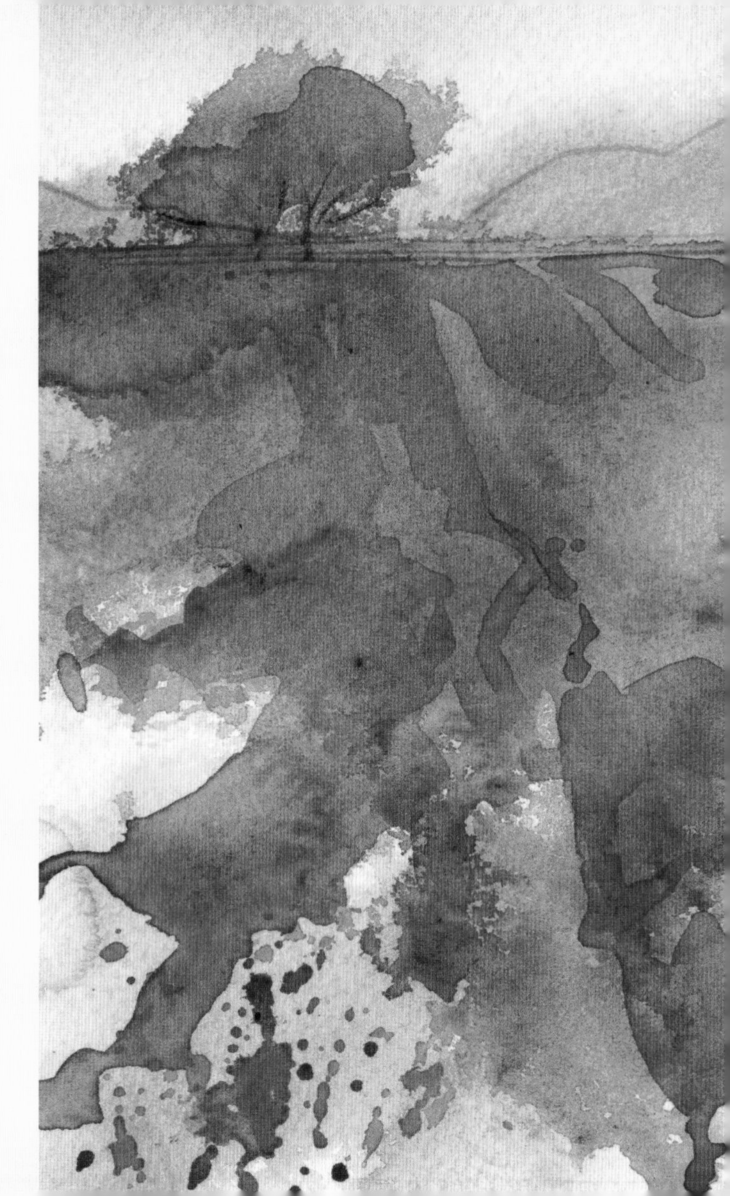

37. I'm still walking. And so are you

When loss happens, the world shifts momentarily. It holds its breath as it adjusts to this loss as nothing goes unmeasured. Almost as if there is a halt to the movement of moon and stars which no one else feels but you. And when it does we have little choice but to keep going, if only to carry on breathing, acknowledging that sunrise follows sunset, and starlight and moonlight still glow behind cloud or shine in the clearest of skies. We cannot stop time. The world will turn in spite of us and at some point we will join in its joyful movement again. Until then, stand still.

We live in a world which has learnt to move too fast, wanting solutions at speed, and showing reluctance at the idea of waiting. Our breath quickens, and adrenaline responds as we prepare to run. But this, this, cannot be forced. We must learn a different way to be. To trust. To wait. And keep waiting until we can begin again.

Until then, as Teilhard de Chardin says, 'trust in the slow work of God'.

38. A connection through grief

In the early days grief was all we knew. As a family we stumbled through the days as best we could. We were still breathing. We had to eat, to walk, to sit. And the enormity of the grief, I realised, kept me connected to Peter in a palpable way. So as time moved on I found that as some of the intensity of the pain lessened, I felt I was losing my connection with him. There was a longing to go back, which seems a strange thing to admit; back into that intense distress, because I felt without it I was losing him. It took me a while to realise this was not the case. Our feelings rose and fell, much like the tides and swell of the sea. If we felt nothing, that was okay. If we wept again, that too was okay. The feeling you and

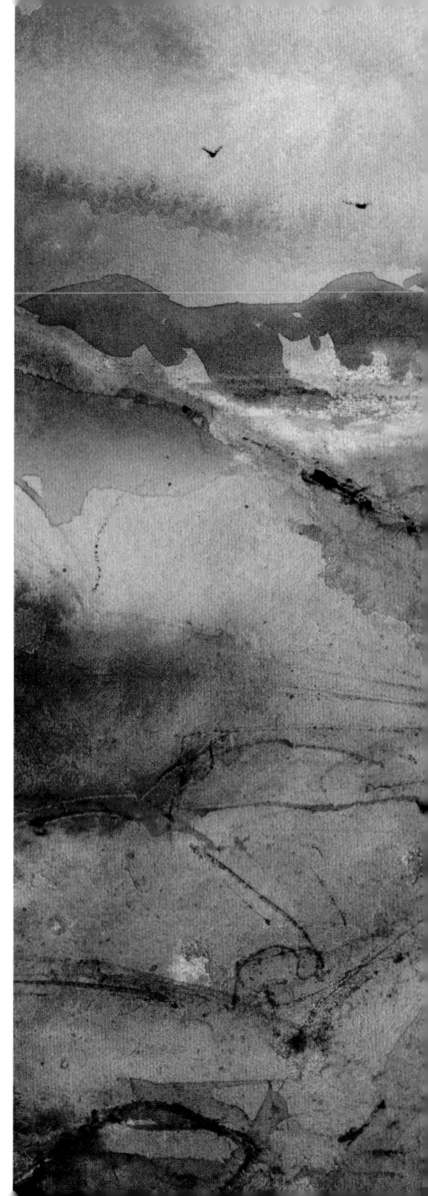

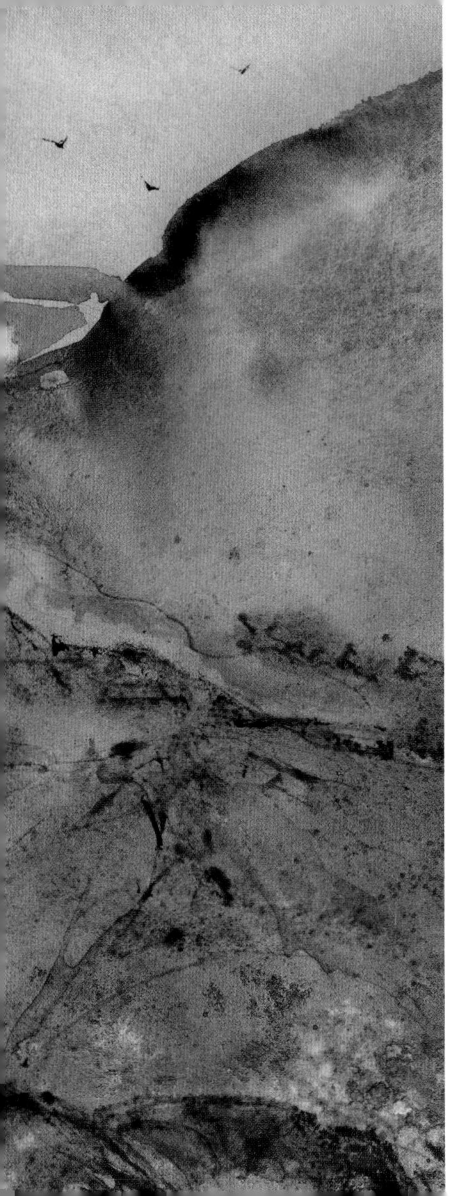

I have right now, that is where we are. There is no use pretending, or trying to run from it. Acceptance brings a gentle relief if only for a short while. And the truth is we do not lose those we grieve for just because we are thinking of something else or immersing ourselves in our work. They are now part of our DNA. Their lives and their love for us have become so deep a part of our ongoing story and our physical being that nothing we can do can deny them. And that comforts me. Regardless of where I am or what I am doing, Peter is there, and always will be. This strange land is becoming more familiar as time passes. This landscape we had no wish to enter is now becoming familiar, for we know there is no going back. Only the horizon before us and the distant pathway behind. Acceptance, surrender, abandoning ourselves to this landscape, it's all the same thing. And it's a kindness to ourselves.

39. It is well with my soul

I have always loved music. Brought up in the church, I have heard, and sung, oh so many, many hymns, and I find now that my tolerance to them is far less than it ever was. I joke that I have a developing allergy to some of them, so when it came to choosing music for Peter's funeral I had to think very carefully as to what he would have liked as well as what we could sing with heartfelt feeling. The easiest of choices was 'It is Well with my Soul', a very familiar and old hymn with a story of great loss behind it. Written by Horatio Spafford, you may well know the story. He lost his two-year-old son whilst living in America, and then much of his business in the Great Chicago Fire of 1871. Two years later, sending his wife and four daughters ahead of him to England, they were in a terrible storm in which all the daughters died. On hearing the news from his wife via a heartbreakingly short telegram, 'Saved alone', he travelled to meet her across the same ocean. He wrote the words to this moving hymn as he passed the area where the storm had hit. I am in awe of anyone who can write such words after so great a loss.

> When peace like a river attendeth my way,
> When sorrows like sea billows roll,
> Whatever my lot, Thou hast taught me to say,
> It is well, it is well with my soul.

I chose the hymn in the hopes that I could, in that moment of pain and farewell, feel the tiniest proportion of trust in that same God. I found I could cry out, 'It is well, it is well with my soul', because in an unexpected way I did believe it was. And I still think of those words, almost eighteen months since, knowing that recognising it is well with our soul does not mean we agree with what has happened to us. How could we in the face of so much sorrow? There is the miracle, that a deeper part of us can say yes, whilst another part is still railing at the way our lives have unfolded. What can I say except therein in lies the mystery of God.

40. Peace will find you

It's a strange thing that in the middle of such ongoing loss and pain we can find peace. Shortly after my father, Eddie Askew, died, I found a journal he had kept since my mother's illness and subsequent death. As with all of his writings, his reflections on the shock and difficulties of the loss of his wife Barbara were poignantly short and searingly honest. He fought the unfairness of it all, he questioned his beliefs, and he showed the depth of his love for her. I wept my way through every page. The great surprise for me was that towards the very end of the journal he wrote these words:

'I am blessed beyond measure.'

He had found what seemed to him an immense measure of deep peace, and there is the miracle we may all experience. Like the starburst moments of small joys, which land like fireflies on the darkness of the path ahead, peace can come in spite of our circumstances. Perhaps I shouldn't be surprised because Jesus talks of the peace available to us, but, if I'm honest, peace in the midst of pain for me has been very much more rare.

Like my father, Peter came to a similar place. A few days before he died, my son Sam and I were sitting with him in the hospice. I can't remember how Sam voiced the question but Peter typed out his slow response. (Since losing his ability to speak ten months after his diagnosis, Peter spoke through a text to voice app).

He said, 'I am at peace.'

My response to this admission was unexpected. I was silent. And, if I'm honest, angrily shocked. I could not speak because inside myself I was screaming at the suffering he was going through, and to hear him say he was at peace seemed like he was announcing he was ready to die. Which he was, yet I was far from ready to let him go. Sitting on the other side of the bed to him, I became horribly aware of a chasm of infinite proportions opening up between us. He was being pulled away whereas I was being forced to stay behind. Now, as I think back, I am unendingly grateful for that moment. In spite of all he had experienced he was at peace. I can't say that I have reached that point myself, or perhaps I have, if acceptance of a situation we cannot change is a sort of peace, for peace can come in all forms. A gentle quiet which rests in the heart, a deeper breath that fills us, or a rush of wind which stops us for a moment, holding us where we are.

Reading the words of Mr Steadfast as he stands on the banks of the river Jordan (from *Pilgrims Progress*, written by John Bunyan in the 17th century), I find myself longing again for that kind of peace.

> "I see myself now at the end of my journey: my toilsome days are ended. I have formerly lived by hearsay and faith, but now I go where I shall live by sight, and shall be with him in whose company I delight myself. I have loved to hear my Lord spoken of; and wherever I have seen the print of his shoe in the earth, there have I coveted to set my foot too. His name to me has

> been like a civet-box; yea, sweeter than all perfumes. His voice to me has been most sweet; his countenance I have more desired than they that have most desired the light of the sun. His word I did gather for my food, and for antidotes against my faintings. He has held me, and I have kept me from mine iniquities; yes my steps he has strengthened in his way."
>
> Now while he was thus in discourse, his countenance changed; his strong men bowed under him after he had said, Take me for I come to thee, he ceased to be seen of them. But glorious it was to see how the upper region was filled with horses and chariots, with trumpeters and pipers, with singers and players on stringed instruments, to welcome the pilgrims as they went up and followed one another in at the beautiful gate of the City.

Pilgrim too had found his peace, and his words were written by a man imprisoned for twelve years because he refused to stop talking publicly about the love of God. We read these words at my father's funeral since it described his own love for God in spite of all.

Those words describe peace in spite of pain, the peace I search for, peace in the midst of pain, peace which sustains within pain. Believe me when I say: however peace comes, you will find it, or rather it will find you.

A Landscape of Grief

Finally, before you go

Thank you for reading this book, but, before you turn the last page and close the book, my prayer for you is that you take a moment to listen to your own heart and look to your dreams. My reasons for this request? Just one. You believe it will never happen to you. You plan when you might step back from work a little. You tell yourself 'Next week I'll have time for the kids.' You think 'Next year we'll make the dream happen.' You promise 'Five years from now I'll change jobs.' And until then you stay busy, putting off the moment of commitment, that decision to make the changes you've been promising yourself for as long as you can remember. But here's the thing. We, none of us, know how long we have left. Nothing is guaranteed. We can hope, we can believe, have faith for better times, going on as we have always done, but please, if you take anything from this journal of our experiences, please, from the depth of my heart, don't wait. If at all possible, set things in place. As Peter would say, just take the first step towards the change your heart is calling out for. You will never regret that you tried, that you began. Disappointment is a coat with deep pockets, so do not walk away from this, your chance at your best life. Fill your life with all that is precious to you and begin now. Be true to yourself, searching always for the goodness and the kindness inside yourself and accepting the kindness of others as gifts from God.

And may the blessings of all that God is, and Her abundant goodness, walk with you as you do. Go gently forwards into your day, and all the days that follow.